HOW TO GROW CARE MANAGE AND USE SAGE FOR PROFIT

Mastering The Art Of Sage - A Strategic Guide To Growing, Nurturing, And Maximizing Profits In Business

LARRY NANCY

ABOUT THIS BOOK

With "How to Grow, Care, Manage, and Use Sage for Profit," you can learn all about how to grow, care for, and use sage to make money. This helpful book takes you step-by-step through the process, starting with an in-depth look at the herb and all of its uses. The book gives you a deep understanding of the benefits of growing sage, both in terms of health and food, as well as from an economic point of view.

Practical advice on starting and maintaining a successful sage cultivation business is given, covering topics like planting methods, soil needs, and the best conditions for growth.

The importance of sage care and maintenance is emphasized, with in-depth information on pruning, irrigation, and pest control. A section on common pests and diseases gives readers the knowledge they need to protect their sage crops.

The book also talks about business, showing people who want to become sage farmers how to expand their businesses. It talks about sage farming as both a hobby and a real business. It has chapters on business planning, marketing strategies, and making the most money from sage products.

"How to Grow, Care, Manage, and Use Sage for Profit" also looks ahead to future innovations and trends in the sage industry, giving readers the tools they need to stay ahead of the curve. This book is a must-read for anyone who wants to get the most out of sage for personal and business use.

CHAPTER ONE
INTRODUCTION TO SAGE

Sage, whose scientific name is Salvia officinalis, is a fragrant and useful herb that has been grown and respected for hundreds of years. This introduction will focus on the many aspects of sage cultivation, highlighting its historical importance and the available different types.

How To Understand How Important Sage Is

Sage is an important herb for more than just cooking. It has spiritual, medical, and symbolic meanings. In cooking, it adds a unique earthy and slightly peppery flavor to many dishes. Sage has also been used medicinally for its possible health benefits, such as its anti-inflammatory and antioxidant properties. Finally, sage has cultural meanings, often linked to purification rituals and co

Historical Significance And Usages In The Past

Looking into the history of sage shows that it has been an important part of many different cultures. Sage was used as medicine by ancient peoples like the Greeks and Romans. Its name, Salvia, comes from the Latin word "salvere," which means "to save" or "heal," which shows that it has a long history of being used for medical purposes. Sage was also used in spiritual practices to ward off evil spirits.

An Overview Of Sage Types

Sage comes in a lot of different types, each with its unique look, taste, and growth habits. Some common types are Garden Sage (Salvia officinalis), Pineapple Sage (Salvia elegans), and Clary Sage (Salvia sclarea). Garden Sage has gray-green leaves and is often used in cooking. Pineapple Sage has a strong pineapple smell that adds a sweet note to both food and decorations.

Making Money By Growing Sage

To grow sage for profit, you need to be smart and plan. First, you need to choose the right spot. Sage does best in well-drained soil with lots of sunlight, so it can be grown in both backyard gardens and larger commercial farms.

You should also choose the right way to propagate the plants based on how big your farm is. Making sure there is enough space between plants for them to grow well and regularly pruning them encourages b

How To Take Care Of And Grow Sage

To keep a sage crop healthy and productive, it's important to water it enough, especially during dry times, because sage likes it well-watered but not soaked. Mulching around the plants helps keep the moisture in, keeps weeds down, and keeps the soil temperature stable.

Regularly checking for pests and diseases is important, and using natural predators or organic remedies can reduce the need for chemicals.

Using Sage To Make Money

Sage is used for more than just cooking, and there are many ways to make money from it. In the culinary world, you can sell fresh or dried sage leaves, as well as value-added products like oils and seasonings infused with sage. In the medicinal world, you can make supplements, teas, and extracts from sage, taking advantage of the herb's supposed health benefits.

Finally, extracting essential oils from some types of sage opens up new ways to make money.

 growing, caring for, managing, and using sage for profit is a complicated process that combines farming, tradition, and business. To be successful in this venture, one must have a deep understanding of the sage's historical significance, its many varieties, and the practical aspects of growing and using it.

By using sustainable methods, taking advantage of the herb's versatility, and staying in touch with market needs, one can

CHAPTER TWO
THE BENEFITS OF GROWING SAGE

The growing of sage has many benefits, including health and medicinal uses, culinary uses with a unique flavor profile, and uses in aromatherapy and other non-culinary areas. It is important to understand these aspects if you want to grow, care for, manage, and ultimately benefit from sage cultivation.

Sage, whose scientific name is Salvia officinalis, is famous for its health and medicinal benefits. The plant has many bioactive compounds, such as rosmarinic acid, flavonoids, and essential oils, which help make it anti-inflammatory, antioxidant, and antimicrobial. Studies have shown that sage extracts may be good for brain function, which could help with the management of neurodegenerative conditions.

Sage is known for having a unique flavor that makes it a mainstay in many different types of food around the world. The herb gives food a strong, earthy taste with light hints of mint and citrus.

It works well with meats, especially chicken and pork, as well as in stuffings, sauces, and soups. Sage's unique smell and taste make it a popular culinary herb that improves the taste of many different dishes.

Sage is useful in more ways than just the kitchen. The essential oils that come from it contain aromatic compounds that are thought to have therapeutic effects on the mind and body.

Using sage in aromatherapy is often linked to lowering stress, improving mood, and clearing the mind. The herb's scent is also thought to have antimicrobial properties, which makes it a useful ingredient in natural cleaning products.

To grow and run a sage cultivation business successfully, you need to pay attention to several things, such as the soil, how much water it needs, and how to keep pests away. Sage grows best in sandy loam soil with a slightly alkaline pH that drains well. It also needs at least six hours of direct sunlight per day. Although sage can survive drought, it needs regular watering during its establishment phase.

For proper care, pruning is an important part of growing sage. Regular pruning helps keep the plant's shape, promotes bushier growth, and keeps it from turning woody. Sage should be harvested strategically, with the leaves tasting best just before they flower. The best way to dry the herb is to keep its essential oils and flavors for a long time. Since sage is a perennial plant, knowing how to take care of it in the winter is also very important.

To make the most money from growing sage, business owners should think about offering a wider range of products. For example, making value-added products like dried sage bundles for smudging, packaged culinary sage blends, and wellness products with essential oils can help reach a larger audience.

Forming partnerships with local markets, health food stores, and wellness practitioners can also help spread the word. Using sustainable and organic methods will not only help your business, but they will also help the environment.

Finally, growing sage is a great way for people who want to combine farming with the health, culinary, and wellness industries. Knowing all of the sage's benefits, from its healing properties and culinary uses to its use in aromatherapy and spiritual practices, is important for growing it successfully and getting into new markets.

CHAPTER THREE
HOW TO BEGIN: GROWING SAGE

Sage (Salvia officinalis) is a fragrant and useful herb that is used in cooking and for its health benefits. If you want to grow sage for profit, you need to know the important things about how to care for, grow, and run your business. In this detailed guide, we'll go over the basic ideas that will help you build a successful sage cultivation business.

Picking The Right Site And Soil

If you want your sage to grow well and produce a lot of leaves, you need to choose the right spot for it. Sage does best in well-drained soils with a pH level between 6.0 and 7.0. It's also important to pick a spot that gets full sunlight since sage needs at least 6 to 8 hours of direct sunlight every day.

A spot with good airflow also helps keep diseases away and encourages strong plant growth. Sage likes sandy loam or loamy soil.

Seeds, cuttings, and transplants are all ways to make plants grow.

Successful propagation is an important part of growing sage for profit. There are several ways to do this, including seeds, cuttings, and transplants. Starting from seeds is the cheapest option, but you have to be patient because germination can take several weeks. Using high-quality seeds and planting them in well-prepared seedbeds can increase germination rates. Cuttings are another popular method that gives faster results. Choose healthy, disease-free stems a

Important Weather And Conditions For Growing

To get a good harvest, you need to know the right climate and growing conditions for sage. Sage does best in Mediterranean climates, but it can survive in a variety of settings.

Once it's established, it's a hardy perennial that can handle drought, but it needs to be watered enough during dry spells, especially in the beginning stages of growth. Sage is tough, but it can't handle frost, so it's important to protect the plants during col

How To Take Care Of And Manage People

To get the most money out of sage, you need to take good care of it and manage it well. Regular pruning is key to making the plants grow bushier, improving airflow, and keeping them healthy.

Sage should be picked when they're at their best, usually before they flower, to get the most essential oils. Drying and storing the herb correctly is also important to keep its flavor and smell. Sage can be attacked by pests like

Using Sage To Make Money

Once the sage crop has been grown and harvested successfully, the next step is to look for different ways to make money.

Sage can be used in many different ways, which makes it marketable in both the wellness and food industries. Selling fresh sage to local markets, grocery stores, or restaurants can be a good way to make money. Drying and packaging sage for retail, either as whole leaves or ground powder, gives you the chance to reach a wider audience.

Making money by growing sage requires a lot of different skills, such as picking the right spot and soil, using good propagation methods, knowing the right growing conditions, and taking good care of and managing the plants. Growing sage successfully requires both scientific knowledge and business sense to take advantage of the many market opportunities this versatile herb offers.

CHAPTER FOUR
TAKING CARE OF AND MAINTAINING SAGE

Sage is a versatile herb with fragrant leaves that is used in cooking and can also be grown for profit. To make sure your sage garden is a success, you need to carefully care for and maintain the plants. This means knowing how to water and irrigation, fertilize the soil, and read the plants' nutritional needs. You also need to know how to prune and harvest them properly.

Tips For Watering And Irrigating

Proper watering and irrigation techniques are very important for the health and productivity of sage plants. Sage likes well-drained soil and can get root rot if it gets too wet, so it's important to find the right balance between giving the plants enough water and keeping them from getting too wet. Watering should be consistent, especially during dry times, but not so much that the soil becomes soaked. Drip irrigation systems are often used.

Fertilizing The Soil And Meeting Its Nutrient Needs

Sage, like many other herbs, does best in soil that is full of nutrients. Fertilization is an important part of sage care and maintenance because it affects not only the plants' growth and vigor but also the smell of the leaves. To find out what nutrients are already in the soil, you should test it before you plant. Then, you can make an informed decision about fertilization. Sage usually does best with well-balanced, organic fertilizers that have a higher concentration of phosphorus to

Techniques For Pruning And Harvesting

Pruning and harvesting techniques are pivotal aspects of sage cultivation that directly influence plant shape, yield, and overall quality. Pruning serves multiple purposes, including shaping the plant for better air circulation, controlling its size, and encouraging bushier growth. For optimal results, it is recommended to commence pruning in the early stages of growth, focusing on removing dead or diseased branches and promoting lateral branching. Harvesting, on the other hand, should be timed appropriately to maximize the concentration of essential oils in the leaves.

The best time to harvest sage is typically before flowering when the essential oil content is at its peak. Employing sharp, clean scissors or shears, practitioners should cut the stems just above a pair of leaves, stimulating new growth and ensuring a continuous harvest. Properly dried and stored sage leaves fetch a higher market value, making these pruning and harvesting techniques crucial for both culinary enthusiasts and commercial cultivators seeking to capitalize on the economic potential of sage cultivation.

As a conclusion, growing sage for profit depends on careful care and maintenance. Watering and irrigation must be carefully managed to avoid water-related problems, and soil fertilization requires a deep understanding of what nutrients the plants need. Pruning and harvesting techniques, when done strategically, improve not only the health of the plants but also the quality and quantity of the harvest.

Pests And Diseases That People Usually Deal With

Sage farming can be profitable if it is done right. This guide goes over all the details of growing, caring for, managing, and using sage for profit, with a focus on how to deal with common pests and diseases.

Diseases And Pests That Are Common

Pests and diseases can make farming, including growing sage, less productive. To keep your sage crop healthy, you need to be able to identify and get rid of common pests like aphids, spider mites, and caterpillars.

Aphids are tiny insects that feed on plant sap; you can tell them apart by their pear-shaped bodies.

Sage can get a lot of different diseases, like powdery mildew, root rot, and fungal infections. Powdery mildew shows up as a white powder on the leaves and hurts photosynthesis and the health of the plant as a whole. Root rot is caused by waterlogged soil and destroys the plant's roots. Fungal infections can cause leaf spots and wilting. You can help the plant stay healthy by using cultural practices.

Organic and chemical-free ways to get rid of pests are becoming more popular in sustainable agriculture. Using these methods will help grow enough sage to meet the demand for organically grown herbs. Organic ways to get rid of pests include using predatory beetles, neem oil, and garlic-based sprays. These methods not only get rid of pests but also keep the environment where the sage is grown in balance.

it is important to know a lot about the common pests and diseases that affect sage to grow it successfully and make money. Using good identification, prevention, and management strategies for these pests and diseases will improve the overall health and quality of sage crops, which will make the sage cultivation industry more profitable.

CHAPTER SIX
SAGE FARMING AND GROWING IT UP

Making Plans For And Designing Your Sage Farm

A thorough analysis of the environment, soil quality, and water availability is necessary for any sage farming project to be successful. Picking the right location is very important, as sage grows best in well-drained soils that get a lot of sunlight. Delineating the cultivation area is also important, keeping in mind the growth potential. Making sure there is enough space between sage plants is important to prevent

Tools and equipment for farming that works well:

Getting the right tools and equipment is very important for getting the most out of sage farming. Mechanization not only cuts down on labor costs but also increases output.

Tractor-mounted cultivators and harvesters make cultivation easier and allow for large-scale operations.

Precision seeding equipment makes sure that plants are spaced evenly, which leads to higher yields. Finally, it's important to use specialized tools for controlling weeds and pests.

Practices For Sustainable Farming

Sustainability is an important part of modern farming, and sage farming is no different. Using sustainable methods not only protects the environment but also makes sure that the sage farming business will be around for a long time. For example, using natural fertilizers and pest control methods in organic farming improves soil health and lowers the impact on the environment. Crop rotation is another sustainable method that keeps soil from being used up and stops the buildup of sage farming needs careful planning and design, smart investments in efficient equipment, and a strong commitment to environmentally friendly methods. If farmers follow these ideas, they can expand their businesses, make the best use of resources, and help the sage industry grow and make money.

CHAPTER SEVEN
PLANNING A BUSINESS WITH SAGE

Sage is a versatile herb that can be used in cooking, medicine, and beauty products, so it needs a well-thought-out business plan to be grown and used for profit. Business planning includes figuring out the purpose and goals of sage cultivation, analyzing market needs, and coming up with plans for long-term growth. This planning process should include a full analysis of resources, market, and competitors.

Researching the market and finding profitable niches:

For sage to grow well, you need to do a lot of market research. This means learning about current market trends, consumer preferences, and profitable niches in the herb industry.

The research should include both domestic and international markets so you can take advantage of global opportunities. Figuring out profitable niches means finding specific parts of the market where sage can grow well and meet unmet needs or preferences.

How To Make A Business Plan

You need to make a detailed business plan if you want the sage cultivation venture to be successful. The business plan should include the enterprise's goals, mission, and vision, as well as its operational aspects, such as growing methods, processing methods, and distribution strategies. To make sure the venture is resilient against risks, the business plan should include financial projections, risk assessments, and backup plans.

Legal Things To Think About And Rules

To follow the rules and lower the risks of growing sage, you need to know about the local, regional, and international laws that govern growing, processing, and distributing herbs. It's also important to follow standards for health and safety, the environment, and agriculture to stay out of trouble with the law. Other important things to remember are to get the right permits and licenses, protect intellectual property, and

 to grow, care for, manage, and make money off of sage, you need to think about business planning, market research, niche identification, and legal issues all at the same time. A well-written business plan is the foundation that guides the cultivation venture towards its goals. Thorough market research helps cultivators find profitable niches and cash in on new trends. At the same time, understanding and following the law are very important.

CHAPTER EIGHT
HOW TO SELL YOUR SAGE PRODUCTS

Building a Brand for Your Sage Products: If you want your sage products to stand out in the market, you need to build a strong brand. A well-established brand not only attracts customers but also builds trust and credibility. To do this, start by figuring out what makes your sage products different from competitors. Then, write an interesting brand story that speaks to your target audience, focusing on the natural and health-promoting benefits of your products.

Online and Offline Marketing Strategies: To effectively market your sage products, a well-rounded approach encompassing both online and offline strategies is essential. In the digital realm, create a user-friendly and visually appealing website that highlights the benefits of your sage products.

Optimize your online presence through search engine optimization (SEO) techniques to ensure that potential customers can easily find your products. Leverage social media platforms to engage with your audience, sharing content that educates them about the uses and benefits of sage. Incorporate influencer marketing to tap into a wider audience and gain credibility. In the offline sphere, participate in trade shows, farmers' markets, and health expos to showcase your sage products and directly connect with consumers. Collaborate with health food stores and local retailers to expand your offline distribution channels. The integration of both online and offline strategies will create a comprehensive marketing plan that maximizes your sage product's exposure and reach.

Connecting with Buyers and Distributors: Building strong connections with buyers and distributors is crucial for the success of your sage products. Identify and target potential buyers, such as retailers, restaurants, and health food stores, who align with your product's values and target audience. Develop professional relationships by providing them with comprehensive information about your sage products, including certifications, quality assurance, and potential profit margins. Offer incentives for initial orders to entice buyers and facilitate the product placement process. Collaborate with distributors who specialize in health and wellness products to ensure widespread availability. Regularly communicate with buyers and distributors to gather feedback, address concerns promptly, and maintain a positive rapport. Establishing a network of reliable partners and fostering open communication channels will contribute to the sustained growth and success of your sage products in the market.

How To Take Care Of Sage Plants?

Understanding the Growth Requirements: If you want to grow sage plants successfully, you need to know exactly what they need to grow. Sage is a hardy perennial herb that does best in well-drained soil with a slightly alkaline pH. For best growth, make sure the plants get at least six to eight hours of sunlight each day. Good airflow is important to keep diseases away, so don't crowd the plants together. Regularly check the soil's moisture level and make sure it's just right.

Correct pruning and harvesting methods are very important for sage plants because they affect both plant health and product quality. Regularly prune the plants to keep their shape, get rid of dead or diseased growth, and encourage new growth. Don't prune too much in the winter to protect the plant from cold stress. Pick the leaves when they taste the best, which is usually right before the plant blooms.

Pest and Disease Management: Sage plants are usually resistant to pests and diseases, but you need to be proactive to avoid problems. Check the plants often for signs of aphids, spider mites, and powdery mildew. Plant garlic and onions next to the sage to naturally keep pests away. Introduce beneficial insects like ladybugs to control aphid populations. If a pest infestation happens, use organic insecticidal soap or neem oil as a last resort.

Using Sage To Make Money

Increasing the Number of Products You Sell: To make the most money, try using sage in more ways than just dried leaves. For example, you could make sage essential oil, which is known for its healing and pleasant smell. You could also make sage-infused oils, vinegar, or spice blends for a wider audience. Finally, you could try making herbal teas or wellness products that use sage's healing properties.

Value-Added Processing and Packaging: Investing in value-added processing and packaging makes your sage products more marketable and raises their perceived value. Try new ways to extract and concentrate sage's beneficial compounds to make high-value extracts or concentrates. Make packaging that is both attractive and informative that highlights the benefits and features of your products. Think about eco-friendly and sustainable packaging options to meet your needs.

Quality Control and Certification: To make sure your sage products do well on the market, you need to follow strict quality control measures and get the right certifications. During the production process, make sure your products are tested for purity, potency, and the absence of contaminants. Follow Good Agricultural Practices (GAP) and Good Manufacturing Practices (GMP) to ensure product quality and safety. Get certifications like o

 carefully taking care of sage plants, using smart marketing strategies, and planning how to use sage products can all make an herbal products business very profitable. Building a strong brand, using a variety of marketing strategies, and getting to know buyers and distributors are all important parts of successful marketing. Knowing the growth requirements and following the right care and management practices are also important.

CHAPTER NINE
USING SAGE PRODUCTS TO MAKE THE MOST MONEY
Adding New Products To Your Line

Diversifying the product line is a smart way to get the most money out of growing and using sage. This means making more sage-based products to appeal to a wider range of market segments and consumer tastes. By doing this, farmers can meet the needs of current customers and attract new ones. To do this, they need to understand the target market and find any gaps in the products they already have.

Ideas For Value-Added Goods And Packaging

Making value-added products from sage increases profits by using the plant's many useful qualities. Value addition involves changing sage into different forms that provide extra benefits, like ease of use, better taste, or longer shelf life.

For example, making sage extracts, tinctures, or concentrates for medical use can meet the growing demand for natural remedies. Also, exploring culinary uses like sa

How To Set Prices To Make Money

To make the most money from sage products, farmers and producers need to come up with good pricing strategies. When setting prices, they need to think about things like production costs, market demand, and perceived value. A cost-plus pricing model, which involves adding a markup to the production cost, is common in agriculture.

But to make the most money, it's important to look at the competition and how customers act.

 making the most money with sage products requires a well-thought-out plan that includes offering a range of products, adding value, and setting fair prices.

Farmers and producers can build a successful and long-lasting business around this fragrant herb by studying the market, using its many uses, and adapting to what customers want.

CHAPTER TEN
INNOVATIONS AND TRENDS FOR THE FUTURE

Keeping Up With Changes In The Industry

To successfully grow sage and sell it for a profit, growers and business owners must stay alert and up-to-date on the constantly changing herbal industry. To stay on top of industry trends, one must constantly watch how markets work, new technologies emerge, and consumer tastes change. For sage cultivation, this means staying up-to-date on new farming techniques, pest control methods, and environmentally friendly farming methods.

Looking For New Ways To Use Sage

As the demand for herbal products continues to rise, finding new ways to use sage could be a good way to make money and grow. Sage has been used traditionally in cooking and medicine, but entrepreneurs can do research and development to find new ways to use it. They might work with researchers, chefs, and experts in different fields to find untapped potential. For example, sage-infused products like teas, essential oils, and

Changing With The Times To Meet Customer Needs

The herbal industry is very competitive, and businesses must be able to adapt to changing consumer tastes. Consumers' behaviors and expectations are always changing, and are affected by things like health trends, cultural shifts, and environmental awareness. For sage growers and businesses, understanding these changes is very important. To do this, they need to do market research, consumer surveys, and talk to their target audiences to find out what their changing tastes are.

CONCLUSION

the journey to growing, caring for, managing, and profiting from sage involves a multifaceted approach that integrates agricultural expertise, innovation, and a keen awareness of consumer dynamics. Keeping abreast of industry trends is foundational, serving as the compass for strategic decision-making and ensuring that growers are not only meeting current demands but also anticipating future needs. Exploring innovative uses for sage is a gateway to differentiation and market expansion, encouraging collaboration and research to unlock the full potential of this versatile herb. Adapting to changing consumer preferences is the linchpin that connects cultivation practices to market success, emphasizing the importance of flexibility and responsiveness. By embodying these principles, stakeholders in the sage industry can not only cultivate a thriving business but also contribute to the sustainability and dynamism of the herbal market at large. The convergence of knowledge, innovation, and consumer-centric strategies is the key to unlocking the full potential of sage cultivation for profitable ventures in the contemporary herbal industry.